Margaret Wise Brown

Four Fur Feet

ILLUSTRATED BY

Woodleigh Marx Hubbard

Hyperion Paperbacks for Children
New York

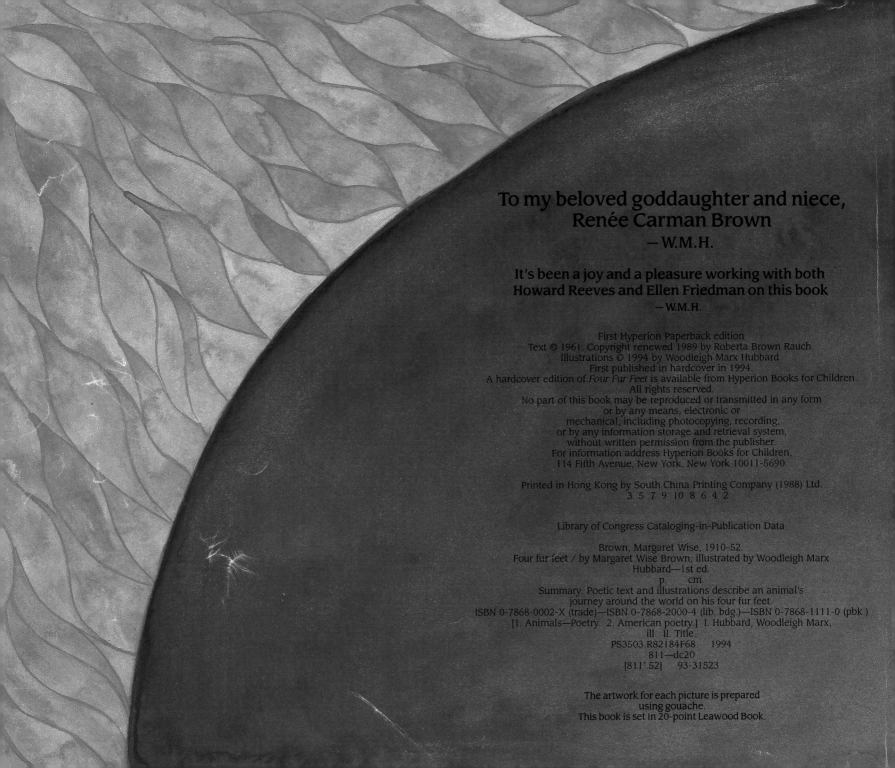

To my beloved goddaughter and niece,
Renée Carman Brown
—W.M.H.

It's been a joy and a pleasure working with both
Howard Reeves and Ellen Friedman on this book
—W.M.H.

First Hyperion Paperback edition
Text © 1961. Copyright renewed 1989 by Roberta Brown Rauch.
Illustrations © 1994 by Woodleigh Marx Hubbard.
First published in hardcover in 1994.
A hardcover edition of *Four Fur Feet* is available from Hyperion Books for Children.
For information address Hyperion Books for Children,
114 Fifth Avenue, New York, New York 10011-5690.

Printed in Hong Kong by South China Printing Company (1988) Ltd.
3 5 7 9 10 8 6 4 2

Library of Congress Cataloging-in-Publication Data

Brown, Margaret Wise, 1910–52.
Four fur feet / by Margaret Wise Brown; illustrated by Woodleigh Marx
Hubbard—1st ed.
p.   cm.
Summary: Poetic text and illustrations describe an animal's
journey around the world on his four fur feet.
ISBN 0-7868-0002-X (trade)—ISBN 0-7868-2000-4 (lib. bdg.)—ISBN 0-7868-1111-0 (pbk.)
[1. Animals—Poetry. 2. American poetry.] I. Hubbard, Woodleigh Marx,
ill. II. Title.
PS3503.R82184F68   1994
811—dc20
[811'.52]   93-31523

The artwork for each picture is prepared
using gouache.
This book is set in 20-point Leawood Book.

FOUR FUR FEET

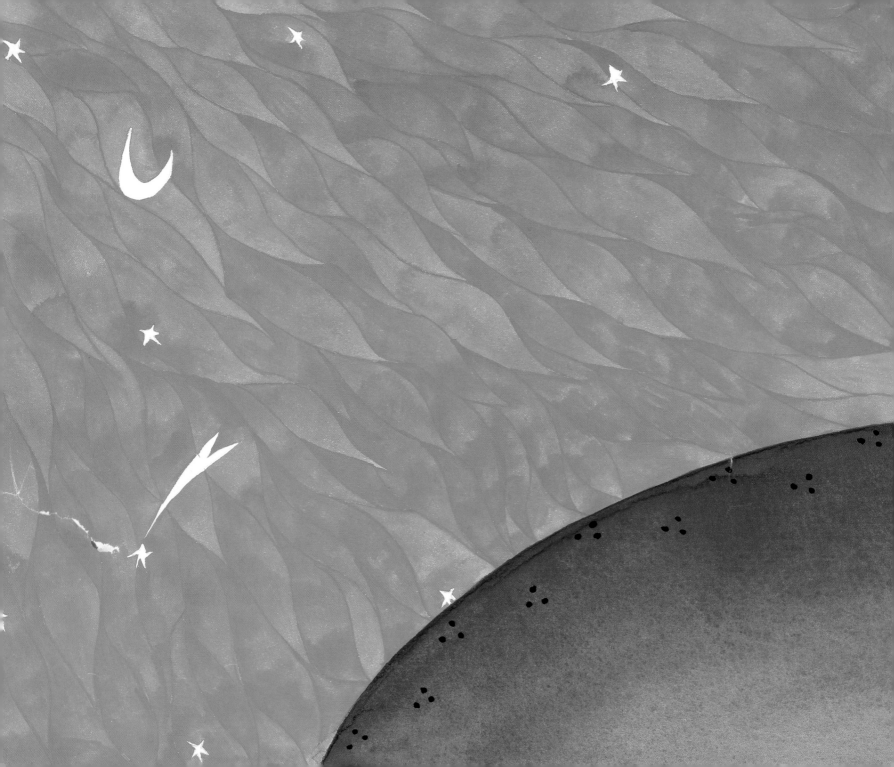

Oh, he walked around the world
on his four fur feet...

Oh, he walked around the world
on his four fur feet,
his four fur feet,
his four fur feet.

And he walked around the world
on his four fur feet
and never made a sound — O.

Oh, he walked along the river on his four fur feet,
his four fur feet, his four fur feet.
He walked along the river on his four fur feet
and heard the boats go toot—O.

Then he walked by the railroad
on his four fur feet,
his four fur feet, his four fur feet.
He walked by the railroad
on his four fur feet
and heard the trains go whoo—O.

Then he walked into the country on his four fur feet,
his four fur feet, his four fur feet.
He walked into the country on his four fur feet
and heard the cows go moo—O.

Then he waded down a stream on his four fur feet,
his four fur feet, his four fur feet.
He waded down a stream on his four fur feet,
and the water was all wet—O.

So he folded up his four fur feet,
his four fur feet, his four fur feet.
So he folded up his four fur feet
and lay down in the grass—O.

And the sun shone down on his four fur feet,
his four fur feet, his four fur feet.
And the sun shone down on his four fur feet
and made them feel all warm—O.

And as he slept he dreamed a dream,
dreamed a dream, dreamed a dream.
And as he slept he dreamed a dream
that all the world was round—O.

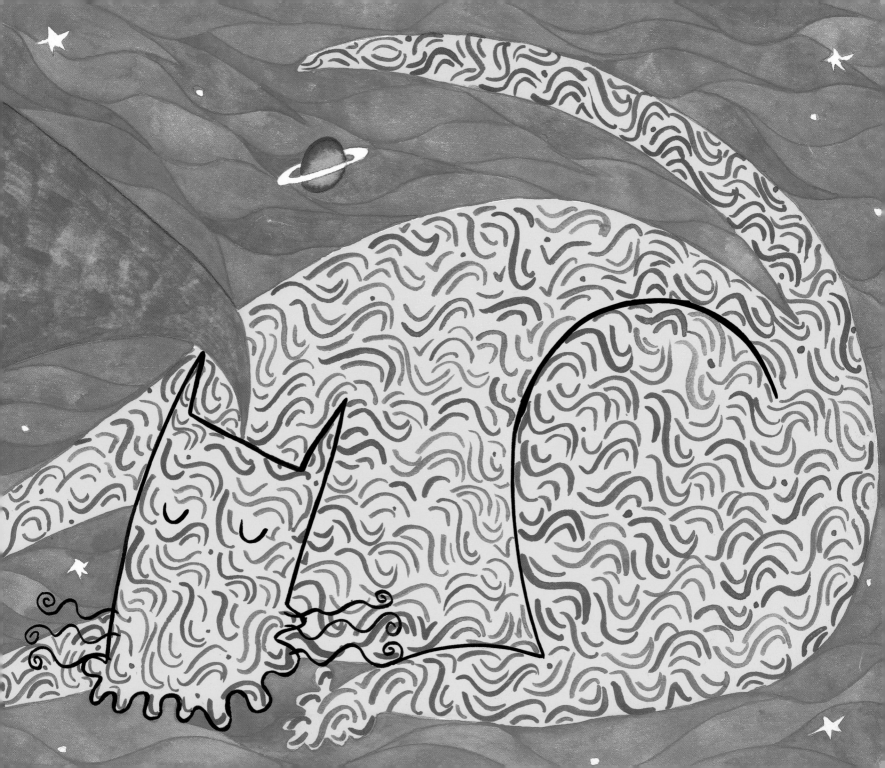

Oh, he walked around the world
on his four fur feet,
his four fur feet, his four fur feet.

And he walked around the world
on his four fur feet

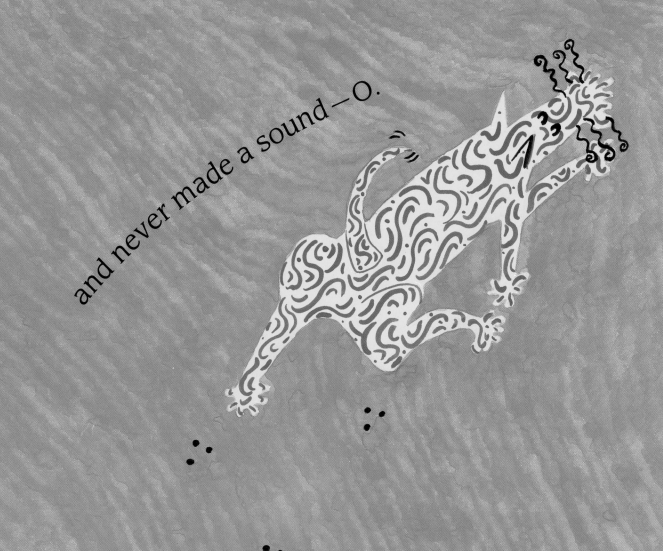

and never made a sound—O.